Vermont

by Patricia K. Kummer
Capstone Press
Geography Department

Consultant:
Michael Sherman
Division of Liberal Studies
Vermont College of Norwich University

CAPSTONE
HIGH/LOW BOOKS
an imprint of Capstone Press
Mankato, Minnesota

8808156

Capstone High/Low Books are published by Capstone Press
818 North Willow Street • Mankato, Minnesota 56001
http://www.capstone-press.com

Library of Congress Cataloging-in-Publication Data
Kummer, Patricia K.
    Vermont/by Patricia K. Kummer (Capstone Press Geography Department).
    p. cm.—(One nation)
    Includes bibliographical references and index.
    Summary: Gives an overview of the state of Vermont, including its history,
geography, people, and living conditions.
    ISBN 0-7368-0121-9
    1. Vermont—Juvenile literature. [1. Vermont.] I. Capstone Press. Geography
Dept. II. Title III. Series.
F49.3.K86 1999
974.3—dc21
                                                                98-31223
                                                                    CIP
                                                                    AC

Editorial Credits
Angela Kaelberer, editor; Timothy Halldin, cover designer and illustrator;
    Sheri Gosewisch and Kimberly Danger, photo researchers

Photo Credits
Archive Photos, 22
Frank S. Balthis, 14
International Stock/Nancy Sanford, cover
Kay Shaw, 18, 24
Lynn M. Stone, 26
One Mile Up, Inc., 4 (top)
Photo Network/Dennis MacDonald, 16
PhotoBank, Inc./Bill Lai, 20; C. D. Benes, 30
Robert McCaw, 5 (top)
Root Resources, 4 (bottom); Root Resources/Ruth A. Smith, 5 (bottom)
Tom Till, 6
Unicorn Stock Photos/Dennis MacDonald, 8; Andre Jenny, 10, 29, 37;
    Ron Holt, 32, 34

Table of Contents

Fast Facts about Vermont

State flag

Location: In the northeastern United States

Size: 9,609 square miles (24,887 square kilometers)

Population: 588,978 (U.S. Census Bureau, 1997 estimate)

Capital: Montpelier

Date admitted to the Union: March 4, 1791; the 14th state

Hermit thrush

Red clover

Largest cities:
Burlington,
Rutland,
South Burlington,
Barre,
Montpelier,
St. Albans,
Winooski,
Newport,
Vergennes

Nickname: The Green Mountain State

State animal:
Morgan horse

State bird:
Hermit thrush

State flower:
Red clover

State tree:
Sugar maple

State song:
"Hail, Vermont!"
by Josephine Hovey Perry

Sugar maple

Chapter 1
Vermont's Covered Bridges

Vermont has more covered bridges per square mile than any other state. Each of these bridges has two long walls and a roof. More than 100 covered bridges cross the state's rivers, creeks, and streams.

Reasons for Covered Bridges
People in Vermont began building covered bridges in the early 1800s. The roofs and walls kept the bridges' wooden floors clear of rain, ice, and snow. This prevented the wood from rotting. Also, horses then were the main form of

Vermont has more than 100 covered bridges.

Vermont's Cornish-Windsor Bridge is the longest covered bridge in the United States.

transportation. People rode horses or used them to pull wagons. Walled bridges made it easier for horses to cross water without becoming afraid. The horses remained calm in the enclosed spaces.

Vermont's first covered bridges served many purposes. Business owners hung posters advertising goods on the bridges' inside walls. Travelers often took shelter within the bridges during storms. Children played games in them. People held picnics inside their walls.

Today, cars and trains travel over many early Vermont bridges. People continue to build covered bridges throughout the state. Some visitors come to Vermont just to take pictures of the covered bridges.

Famous Covered Bridges

Pulp Mill Bridge is Vermont's oldest covered bridge. It was built between 1808 and 1820. The bridge crosses Otter Creek between Middlebury and Weybridge. Today, people still drive cars across this bridge.

The Cornish-Windsor Bridge is the longest covered bridge in the United States. It is 449 feet (137 meters) long. This bridge crosses the Connecticut River. It connects Cornish, New Hampshire, and Windsor, Vermont.

The Scott Bridge is in West Townshend, Vermont. This is the longest covered bridge within the state. It is 277 feet (84 meters) long. This bridge crosses the West River.

Vermont's shortest and newest bridge is Kent's Corner Bridge. It was built in 1994 and is only 22 feet (7 meters) long. Kent's Corner Bridge is a private bridge on a farm near Calais.

Chapter 2
The Land

Vermont is in the northeastern United States. It is one of the six New England states. Two other states in this region border Vermont. These are Massachusetts and New Hampshire. The Connecticut River forms Vermont's border with New Hampshire.

New York borders Vermont to the west. Lake Champlain also forms part of the western border. The Canadian province of Quebec borders Vermont to the north.

Vermont has several kinds of land. Mountains rise in the middle and southwest. The low Piedmont region spreads across the eastern part of Vermont. Valleys lie in the west.

Mount Mansfield is Vermont's highest point.

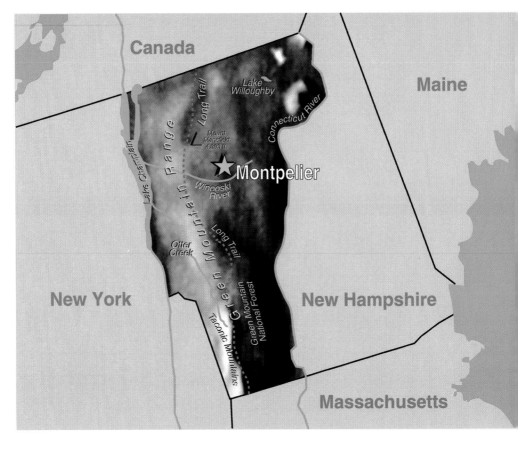

Vermont's Mountains

Mountains cover much of Vermont. There are two mountain ranges in the state. These are the Green Mountains and the Taconic Mountains.

The Green Mountains stretch through Vermont from north to south. This is the state's best-known area. Vermont's nickname is the Green Mountain State. Mount Mansfield is in the northern Green Mountains. It is Vermont's highest point. Mount

Mansfield rises 4,393 feet (1,339 meters) above sea level. Sea level is the average surface level of the world's oceans.

Green Mountain National Forest covers the southern Green Mountains. Sugar maple, hemlock, and spruce trees grow in this forest.

The Taconic Mountains are in far southwestern Vermont. Fast-moving rivers flow through these mountains. Large marble and slate deposits lie within these mountains. These natural layers of stone are found in the ground.

Hills are located in northeastern Vermont. This area is called the Northern Highlands. These hills actually are part of the White Mountains of New Hampshire. Forests cover much of these hills.

The Vermont Piedmont

The state's largest region is the Vermont Piedmont. This region stretches east of the Green Mountains to the Connecticut River. Piedmont means "at the foot of the mountains." Low hills cover Vermont's western Piedmont.

The Connecticut River Valley is in the eastern Piedmont. This land is good for farming.

Vermont's lowest point is along Lake Champlain.

The Vermont and Champlain Valleys

The Valley of Vermont is in southwestern Vermont. It lies between the Green and Taconic Mountains. Large limestone and marble deposits are in this valley.

The Champlain Valley lies in northwestern Vermont between Lake Champlain and the Green Mountains. Much of Vermont's farmland is located in the valley. Vermont's lowest point is along Lake Champlain. This land is 95 feet (29 meters) above sea level.

14

Rivers and Lakes

Otter Creek is the longest river in Vermont. It is 100 miles (161 kilometers) long. Otter Creek begins in the southern Green Mountains and flows north. The Lamoille and Winooski Rivers flow west through the northern Green Mountains. All three rivers empty into Lake Champlain.

More than 400 lakes and ponds are located throughout Vermont. Lake Champlain is the sixth largest freshwater lake in the United States. It is 120 miles (193 kilometers) long and 12 miles (19 kilometers) wide. Parts of Lake Champlain also are located in New York and Quebec.

Climate

Vermont has long, cold winters and short, mild summers. Vermont's average January temperature is 17 degrees Fahrenheit (-8 degrees Celsius). The average July temperature is 71 degrees Fahrenheit (22 degrees Celsius).

Different areas of the state receive different amounts of rain and snow. The Champlain Valley receives about 32 inches (81 centimeters) of rain each year. Vermont's mountains can receive as much as 150 inches (381 centimeters) of snow.

Chapter 3
The People

Vermont has 588,978 people (U.S. Census Bureau, 1997 estimate). This is the third-smallest population of all the states. Only Alaska and Wyoming have fewer people. But Vermont is one of the fastest growing northeastern states. Between 1990 and 1997, the state gained about 26,000 people.

About 68 percent of Vermonters live in rural areas. These areas include farms and small towns. No other state has a higher percentage of people living in rural areas.

The largest number of Vermonters live along Lake Champlain. Many others live in the Vermont and Connecticut River Valleys. Few

Vermont is the state with the highest percentage of people living in rural areas.

Brandon is one of Vermont's 242 towns.

people live in northeastern Vermont. That area is covered by thick forests.

Cities and Towns

Vermont has nine cities and 242 towns. Vermonters have held town meetings since the 1700s. The meetings are on the first Tuesday of March. The townspeople gather in town halls or in schools. They elect the town officials for the next year. The townspeople also vote on local matters. They might decide to build roads or to repair covered bridges.

Vermont's European Background
Many Vermonters can trace their families back to early European settlers. During the 1700s, most Vermonters had English, Scottish, German, or Dutch backgrounds. Many of these settlers moved to Vermont from the Massachusetts, New Hampshire, and New York colonies. They built farms and raised sheep and cattle.

In the 1800s, French-speaking people from Canada moved to Vermont. Some settled on farms. Others found work in Vermont's lumber mills.

Thousands of people also came directly from Europe during the 1800s. Irish and English workers found jobs building railroads and working in copper mines near Ely. Italians carved marble in Proctor and granite in Barre. Spanish stone cutters also found work in Barre. Welsh slate cutters worked in Poultney. Swedish farmers settled near Wilmington and Weston.

Today, almost 97 percent of Vermonters have European backgrounds. People with English and

Asian Americans make up nearly 1 percent of Vermont's population.

French backgrounds make up Vermont's largest population groups.

Native Americans

About 1,700 Native Americans live in Vermont. They make up about 0.3 percent of the state's population. The Abenaki people are Vermont's largest Native American group. The Abenaki once occupied most of Vermont. European settlers and fur traders forced most

Abenaki to give up their land. Some fled to Canada. Today, many Abenaki live in Swanton near Lake Champlain. Others live along the Connecticut River.

Since the 1970s, the Abenaki have worked to regain land in Vermont. The Abenaki also want the U.S. government to recognize them as an official tribe. This would give the Abenaki greater land, hunting, and fishing rights under U.S. government laws.

Other Ethnic Groups

About 5,700 Hispanic Americans live in Vermont. They make up about 1 percent of the state's population.

About 5,300 Asian Americans live in Vermont. They make up about 0.9 percent of the state's population. Many of Vermont's Asian Americans came from South Korea, Taiwan, and India.

About 3,500 African Americans live in Vermont. They make up about 0.6 percent of the state's population.

Chapter 4
Vermont History

People first arrived in what is now Vermont about 12,000 years ago. In the 1300s, three groups of Native American people settled in the area. They were the Abenaki, the Mahican, and the Pennacook. They all spoke the Algonquian language. Around 1500, the Iroquois people moved into the area. They forced many of the other Native Americans to leave. Most of those who stayed were Abenaki.

France and Great Britain Claim Vermont
In 1609, explorer Samuel de Champlain claimed what is now Vermont for France. Explorers from Great Britain claimed land in

In 1609, explorer Samuel de Champlain claimed what is now Vermont for France.

Ethan Allen's home still stands near Burlington.

what is now North America as well. Between 1607 and 1732, Great Britain settled 13 colonies in North America.

Between 1689 and 1763, France and Great Britain fought for control of North America. In 1763, Britain gained control of land east of the Mississippi River. This included the area that is now Vermont.

The New Hampshire Grants

Before 1763, the New Hampshire and New York colonies claimed what is now Vermont. The governors of both colonies sold land in the area to people in their colonies. At that time, people called what is now Vermont "the New Hampshire Grants." In 1764, King George III of England ruled that the New Hampshire Grants belonged to the New York colony. This rule affected settlers who had received land from New Hampshire. They had to pay New York for their land or leave.

A group of settlers who wanted to keep their land fought the New Yorkers. These settlers called themselves the Green Mountain Boys. Ethan Allen was their leader. The fight lasted from 1770 to 1775. The Green Mountain Boys kept the New Yorkers from taking their land.

Revolutionary War and Statehood

In 1775, the Revolutionary War (1775–1783) began. During the war, colonists fought for their independence from Great Britain. The Green Mountain Boys joined the fight. In 1775, they captured two British forts in New York. In 1777, they helped win the Battle of Bennington.

People in the New Hampshire Grants formed their own state in 1777. They called it the "Free and Independent State of Vermont." The

Dairy farming has been a leading Vermont business since the 1800s.

state's name came from two French words, "vert" and "mont." Together, these words mean "green mountain."

In 1783, the colonies won the Revolutionary War. In 1791, Vermont became the 14th state.

Early Industry and Farming

In the early 1800s, potash was one of Vermont's leading products. This chemical is made from wood ash. Potash was used to dye wool and make soap and glass. Vermonters shipped potash to England and other countries in Europe.

Potash stopped being an important product in the 1820s. Manufacturing changed and potash was no longer used.

Vermonters also grew crops or raised sheep for their wool. But many crops did not grow well in Vermont's rocky soil and cool climate. Wool prices dropped when farmers in western states started raising sheep on large ranches in the 1850s.

Many Vermont farmers then started raising dairy cows. Dairy farming soon became one of Vermont's leading businesses.

Slavery and the Civil War
By the 1850s, slavery divided the country. Vermont had outlawed slavery in 1777. Later, all other Northern states also outlawed slavery. But slavery was allowed in the South.

In 1860 and 1861, 11 Southern states left the United States. They formed the Confederate States of America. This led to the Civil War (1861–1865). About 34,000 Vermonters fought for the United States. In 1865, the United States won the war. Slavery was outlawed in every state.

Growth of Manufacturing and Quarrying
In the late 1800s, manufacturing became important in Vermont. Factories in Bellows Falls

and Springfield made guns and tools. Other factories in St. Johnsbury and Rutland made scales. Brattleboro factories made reed organs.

Quarrying also became a big business during the late 1800s. Quarry workers dig or cut stone from the ground. Workers cut granite from quarries near Barre. Marble cutters worked near Proctor. People cut slate in Poultney.

World Wars and the Great Depression

In 1917, the United States entered World War I (1914–1918). About 15,000 Vermonters fought in the war. Vermont factories made tools and machines used to fight the war.

Many people faced financial problems during the Great Depression (1929–1939). Many Vermont factories and lumber mills closed. In 1933, the U.S. government started the New Deal. Programs in the New Deal provided jobs. People built dams, parks, mountain trails, and ski slopes.

In 1941, the United States entered World War II (1939–1945). About 50,000 Vermonters fought in the war. Vermont's tool factories again made war supplies. Shelburne Shipyards built patrol torpedo boats. These efforts all helped the United States and its allies win the war.

The largest granite quarries in the United States are near Barre, Vermont.

Recent Growth

Vermont's population is increasing rapidly. Since 1950, the state has gained almost 200,000 people.

Population growth can lead to pollution. Vermont's leaders have worked to prevent this problem. A 1970 law protects the environment from pollution caused by businesses. A 1988 law requires Vermont's towns to preserve farmland and forests.

Vermont's laws are working. Today, Vermont is one of the cleanest states.

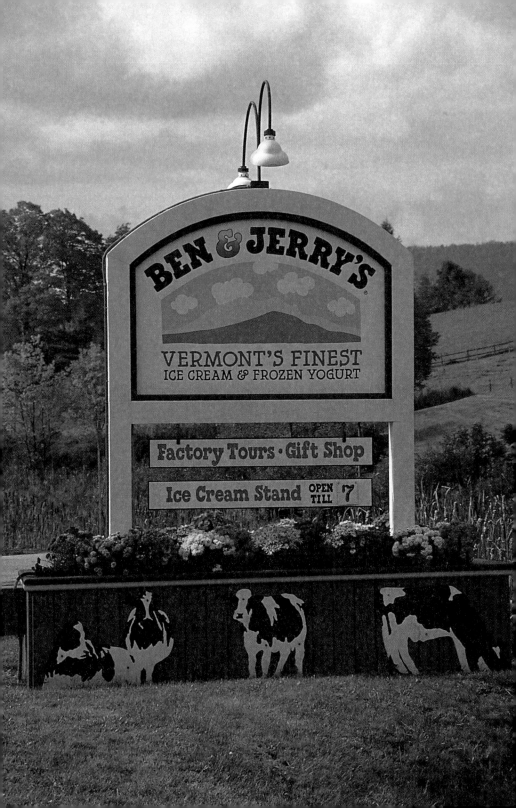

Chapter 5
Vermont Business

Manufacturing is Vermont's single largest business. But service businesses are Vermont's largest combined business. Service businesses include tourism, realty, and government. Farming, mining, and forestry are other important Vermont businesses.

Manufacturing
Vermont's leading manufactured product is computer parts. International Business Machines (IBM) has factories near Burlington.

Many food products also are made in Vermont. Cabot Creamery in Cabot makes many kinds of cheese. Ben & Jerry's Homemade makes more than 50 ice cream products in Waterbury.

Ben & Jerry's Homemade is located in Waterbury.

Vermont produces more maple syrup than any other state.

Service Businesses

Tourism is one of Vermont's largest service businesses. In 1891, Vermont was the first state to establish a state tourism office. Each year, tourists spend more than $2 billion in Vermont.

Vermont's realty businesses have increased in recent years. These businesses buy and sell land, homes, and other buildings.

Many Vermonters work for state or local governments. Some work in state parks or the Green Mountain National Forest.

Agriculture

Vermont does not have as many farms as it once had. But agriculture still is an important business in the state. Milk is Vermont's leading farm product.

Many people in Vermont grow maple trees for sap. In March, they collect and boil the sap to make maple sugar and syrup. Vermont produces more maple syrup than any other state.

Vermont also has many Christmas tree farms. Farmers cut down the trees and ship them all over the United States.

Large crops of apples grow in the Champlain Valley. Hay and corn are other important crops.

Mining and Forestry

Granite is Vermont's leading mined product. The largest granite quarries in the United States are near Barre. Vermont also has large marble and slate quarries.

Forests cover about 77 percent of Vermont. Many logging businesses are located in northeastern Vermont. The trees are used to make paper and furniture.

Chapter 6
Seeing the Sights

People visit Vermont throughout the year. In the fall, visitors come to see the colorful leaves on Vermont's trees. Vermonters call these visitors "leaf peepers." In the winter, Vermont's mountains attract skiers from across the United States. Vermont's small towns hold maple sugar festivals in the spring. In the summer, many Vermonters and visitors hike, bike, boat, and fish.

The Long Trail
The Long Trail is a hiking path. It winds 270 miles (435 kilometers) through the Green Mountains. Vermonters built this mountain trail between 1910 and 1928. It begins in

Many visitors come to see Vermont's colorful leaves each fall.

southwestern Vermont at the Massachusetts border. The trail ends near Jay Peak at the Canadian border.

Northwestern Vermont

The city of Burlington lies along Lake Champlain. Visitors can tour the Ethan Allen Homestead in Burlington.

Shelburne is south of Burlington. The Shelburne Museum attracts many visitors. The museum looks like a New England village in the early 1800s. Most of its 37 buildings once stood in towns throughout New England. Workers moved the buildings to the museum's grounds.

Stowe is east of Burlington. The Mount Mansfield Gondola is near this popular ski town. The gondola is an enclosed cable car that carries people to the top of Mount Mansfield. In the winter, skiers ride the gondola to the slopes. In the summer, mountain bikers take bicycles up the mountain on the gondola.

Northeastern Vermont

Northeastern Vermont is known for thick forests and clear lakes. Lake Willoughby's sandy beaches and good fishing draw many visitors.

A round barn welcomes visitors to Shelburne Museum.

St. Johnsbury is south of Lake Willoughby.
The Fairbanks Museum and Planetarium is in
St. Johnsbury. Visitors learn about science and
natural history from the museum's exhibits.
Visitors also watch images from space projected
on the planetarium's curved ceiling.

East-Central Vermont

Before 1805, Vermont did not have a permanent
state capital. The state's legislature met in
different towns around the state. Montpelier has
been Vermont's capital since 1805. The first

capitol building was torn down in the 1830s. Fire destroyed the second capitol in 1857. Vermonters built the current capitol building in 1859. They built it with Vermont granite and marble.

The Vermont Historical Society museum is in Montpelier. This museum's exhibits help visitors learn about Vermont's history.

Plymouth Notch is south of Montpelier. Visitors tour President Calvin Coolidge's boyhood home there.

West-Central Vermont

The Morgan Horse Farm is in Weybridge. Morgan horses are named for Vermonter Justin Morgan. In the 1790s, Morgan owned the first horse in the breed. People value these horses for their beauty, strength, and gentle nature. Today, visitors watch trainers teach Morgans to carry people on their backs and to pull carriages.

Pittsford is south of Middlebury. Pittsford is home to the New England Maple Museum and Maple Market. Visitors at the museum watch workers make maple syrup from maple sap.

Southern Vermont

Bennington is the home of the Bennington Battle Monument. The monument is 306 feet (93 meters) tall. It honors Vermonters who won the Revolutionary War Battle of Bennington in 1777.

The town of Bellows Falls is on the Connecticut River in southeastern Vermont. Native Americans lived in this area about 1,000 years ago. They carved pictures called petroglyphs in rocks along the Connecticut River. Visitors can still see these drawings today.

Vermont Time Line

10,000 B.C.—The first people settle in what is now Vermont.

A.D. 1300—Abenaki, Mahican, and Pennacook people move into what is now Vermont.

1609—Explorer Samuel de Champlain claims what is now Vermont for France.

1690—English colonists from New York build a fort near what is now Addison.

1724—English colonists from Massachusetts build the area's first permanent European settlement near what is now Brattleboro.

1749—New Hampshire's governor creates the New Hampshire Grants by selling land in what is now Vermont to people in his colony.

1763—Great Britain gains control of what is now Vermont at the end of the French and Indian War (1754—1763).

1764—King George III of England rules that the area that is now Vermont belongs to New York.

1770—Ethan Allen helps organize the Green Mountain Boys.

1777—The Free and Independent State of Vermont is formed.

1791—Vermont becomes the 14th U.S. state.

1805—Montpelier becomes Vermont's permanent capital.

1881—Vermont native Chester Arthur becomes the 21st president of the United States.

1923—Vermont native Calvin Coolidge becomes the 30th president of the United States.

1941—Vermont declares its entry into World War II three months before the United States enters the war.

1954—Vermonter Consuelo Bailey becomes the first U.S. woman elected lieutenant governor.

1970—Vermont's legislature passes the Environmental Control Law to protect the environment from pollution.

1984—Madeleine Kunin becomes the first woman elected governor of Vermont.

1992—Vermont's supreme court rules against the Abenaki claim to land in Vermont.

1997—Vermonter Jody Williams and the International Campaign to Ban Landmines receive the Nobel Peace Prize.

Famous Vermonters

Ethan Allen (1738–1789) Patriot who helped organize the Green Mountain Boys (1770–1775); born in what is now Connecticut; moved to the area that is now Vermont in 1769.

Chester Arthur (1829–1886) Politician who became vice president of the United States in 1881; became the 21st president (1881–1885) when President James Garfield died in office; born in Fairfield.

Ben Cohen (1951–) and **Jerry Greenfield** (1951–) Business owners who co-founded the ice cream company Ben & Jerry's Homemade (1978); both born in New York and moved to Vermont in the late 1970s.

Calvin Coolidge (1872–1933) Politician who became vice president of the United States (1921–1923); became the 30th president (1923–1929) when President Warren Harding died in office; born in Plymouth Notch.

Katherine Paterson (1932–) Children's book author who won Newbery Awards for *Bridge to Terabithia* (1978) and *Jacob Have I Loved* (1981); born in China and moved to Barre in 1964.

Homer St. Francis (1935–) Chief of the Abenaki Nation who has worked to regain land in Vermont for his people; born in Swanton.

Alexander Twilight (1795–1857) Educator and politician who became the United States' first African American college graduate and state legislator; born in Corinth.

Maria von Trapp (1905–1987) Author and musician who wrote *The Story of the Trapp Family Singers*; the book was made into the movie *The Sound of Music*; born in Austria and moved to Stowe in 1942.

Jody Williams (1950–) Peace activist who helped found the International Campaign to Ban Landmines (1991–); awarded the Nobel Peace Prize (1997); born in Rutland.

Words to Know

Abenaki (a-buh-NAH-kee)—a Native American group living in northern New England and Quebec

deposit (di-POZ-it)—a natural layer of rock, sand, or minerals found in the ground

gondola (GON-duh-luh)—an enclosed car that travels high above the ground along a cable

grant (GRANT)—a gift such as land or money given for a particular purpose; the land that is now Vermont was once called "the New Hampshire Grants."

petroglyph (PEH-trah-glif)—a picture or word carved on a rock

planetarium (plan-uh-TAIR-ee-uhm)—a building where visitors see images from space projected on a curved ceiling

quarry (KWOR-ee)—a place where people dig or cut stone from the ground

recognize (REK-uhg-nize)—to accept as official or give official rights to

To Learn More

Elish, Dan. *Vermont*. Celebrate the States. New York: Benchmark Books, 1997.

Fradin, Dennis Brindell. *Vermont*. From Sea to Shining Sea. Chicago: Children's Press, 1993.

Pelta, Kathy. *Vermont*. Hello U.S.A. Minneapolis: Lerner Publications, 1994.

Thompson, Kathleen. *Vermont*. Portrait of America. Austin, Texas: Raintree Steck-Vaughn, 1996.

Internet Sites

Discover Vermont
http://www.discover-vermont.com

Excite Travel: Vermont, United States
http://city.net/countries/united_states/vermont

State of Vermont Home Page
http://www.state.vt.us

Travel.org—Vermont
http://travel.org/vermont.html

Vermont Historical Society
http://www.state.vt.us/vhs

Vermont Only: Vermont Covered Bridges
http://www.vtonly.com/bridges.htm

Vermont Traveler's Guide
http://www.travel-vermont.com

Useful Addresses

Ethan Allen Homestead
1 Ethan Allen Homestead, Suite 2
Burlington, VT 05401-1141

President Calvin Coolidge State Historic Site
P.O. Box 247
Plymouth Notch, VT 05056

Shelburne Museum
P.O. Box 10
Shelburne, VT 05482-0010

**Vermont Department of Tourism
and Marketing**
6 Baldwin Street, Drawer 33
Montpelier, VT 05633-1301

Vermont Historical Society
109 State Street
Montpelier, VT 05609-0901

Index